D0794617

Math Counts

Children's Press®
An Imprint of Scholastic Inc.

About This Series

In keeping with the major goals of the National Council of Teachers of Mathematics, children will become mathematical problem solvers, learn to communicate mathematically, and learn to reason mathematically by using the series Math Counts.

Pattern, Shape, and *Size* may be investigated first—in any sequence.

Sorting, Counting, and *Numbers* may be used next, followed by *Time, Length, Weight,* and *Capacity.*

—Ramona G. Choos, Professor of Mathematics,
Senior Adviser to the Dean of Continuing Education, Chicago State University;
Sponsor for Chicago Elementary Teachers' Mathematics Club

Author's Note

Mathematics is a part of a child's world. It is not only interpreting numbers or mastering tricks of addition or multiplication. Mathematics is about ideas. These ideas have been developed to explain particular qualities such as size, weight, and height, as well as relationships and comparisons. Yet all too often the important part that an understanding of mathematics will play in a child's development is forgotten or ignored.

Most adults can solve simple mathematical tasks without the need for counters, beads, or fingers. Young children find such abstractions almost impossible to master. They need to see, talk, touch, and experiment.

The photographs and text in these books have been chosen to encourage talk about topics that are essentially mathematical. By talking, the young reader can explore some of the central concepts that support mathematics. It is on an understanding of these concepts that a student's future mastery of mathematics will be built.

—Henry Pluckrose

Math Counts

By Henry Pluckrose

Mathematics Consultant: Ramona G. Choos,
Professor of Mathematics

Children's Press®

An Imprint of Scholastic Inc.

Do you ever wonder what words mean? This is a toy bear. It is so big that it would be hard to carry.

This baby elephant is bigger than the toy bear,
but is smaller than its mother.
The mother elephant is the biggest of them all.

This is a toy car.
How do you know that it is too small to carry people?

This car looks almost as small as the toy car.
How can you tell that it is bigger?

This is a van.
Do you think it is bigger
or smaller than the car?

This is a double-decker bus. It carries more than 50 people. It is bigger than the car and the van. It is the biggest vehicle.

To know the size of things
we need to have something to measure them against.
These wheels could be any size.

How do you know
that this wheel is enormous?

It is hard to guess how large this model might be. Is it big—or is it small?

We know that this dinosaur is very big.

These fruits are different sizes.
Which is the biggest? Which is the smallest?

These toy bears are not the same size.
Which is bigger? Which is smaller?

Sometimes we need to arrange things in size order. These jars are different sizes.

Now they are arranged by size.
The biggest jar is on the left.
The smallest jar is on the right.

We use the words *big* and *small* to describe the size of things.

A rabbit is bigger
than a hamster,

but smaller than a pony.

A pony is a big animal, but it is smaller than a horse.

The words *big* and *small* help us compare one thing with another. A coat can be too big

or too small.
Is the girl too big
for the coat,
or is the coat too small
for the girl?

When we buy shoes, we have to make sure that they are the right size

for the person who is going to wear them.

Sometimes we need to make
things appear larger
so that we can see them more easily.
A hornet is a very small creature.
Enlarged, it looks like this.

These are raindrops on a leaf.
They have also been enlarged.

Sometimes things seem to be smaller than they really are. This airplane looks quite small when it is high in the sky.

On the ground, it looks much bigger.

How do you know that this house
is big enough for you to live in,

and that this house has been built for dolls?
What is the biggest thing you can think of?
What is the smallest?

Index

Reader's Guide

Visit this Scholastic Web site to download the Reader's Guide for this series:
www.factsfornow.scholastic.com Enter the keywords **Math Counts**

Library of Congress Cataloging-in-Publication Data
Names: Pluckrose, Henry, 1931- author. | Choos, Ramona G., consultant.
Title: Size/by Henry Pluckrose; mathematics consultant, Ramona G. Choos,
Professor of Mathematics.
Other titles: Math counts.
Description: Updated edition. | New York, NY: Children's Press, an imprint of Scholastic Inc., [2018] | Series: Math counts |
Includes index.
Identifiers: LCCN 2017061280| ISBN 9780531175125 (library binding) | ISBN 9780531135211 (pbk.)
Subjects: LCSH: Size perception—Juvenile literature. | Size judgment—Juvenile literature. | Measurement—Juvenile literature.
Classification: LCC BF299.S5 P59 2018 | DDC 153.7/52—dc23
LC record available at https://lccn.loc.gov/2017061280

Copyright © The Watts Publishing Group, 2018
Printed in Heshan, China 62

Scholastic Inc., 557 Broadway, New York, NY 10012.

1 2 3 4 5 6 7 8 9 10 R 28 27 26 25 24 23 22 21 20 19

Credits: Photos ©: cover: Shavel Aksana/Shutterstock; 1: Shavel Aksana/Shutterstock; 3: Shavel Aksana/Shutterstock; 4: klyots/Shutterstock; 5: Ana Gram/Shutterstock; 6: Ocusfocus/Dreamstime; 7: Bike_Maverick/Getty Images; 8: Grafissimo/iStockphoto; 9: Dallas Kilponen/Bloomberg/Getty Images; 10 brass gears: robas/Getty Images; 10 rusty gears: GLYPHstock/iStockphoto; 10 wagon wheel: Free Oscillation/Shutterstock; 10 truck tire: forest badger/Shutterstock; 10 bike tire: graja/Shutterstock; 10 bottom orange hub tire: Realchemyst/Shutterstock; 10 white tire: Bildagentur Zoonar GmbH/Shutterstock; 10 tractor wheel: Anatoliy Kosolapov/Shutterstock; 10 magenta tire: Guas/Shutterstock; 10 top orange hub tire: XIE WENHUI/Shutterstock; 10 white wheel: studio BM/Shutterstock; 10 green hub tire: Denis Churin/Shutterstock; 11: Leena Yla-Lyly/Folio Images/Getty Images; 12: metha1819/Shutterstock; 13: metha1819/Shutterstock; 14: duescreatius1/iStockphoto; 15: Jeanette Dietl/Shutterstock; 16-17 jars: Bianca Alexis Photography; 16-17 table: nuwatphoto/Shutterstock; 18: sam74100/iStockphoto; 19: khilagan/iStockphoto; 20: Littlekidmomen/Shutterstock; 21: smereka/Shutterstock; 22: Bianca Alexis Photography; 23: Bianca Alexis Photography; 24: RTimages/iStockphoto; 25: Biddiboo/Getty Images; 26: Antagain/iStockphoto; 27: Waroranger/Shutterstock; 28: ILYA AKINSHIN/Shutterstock; 29: Monty Rakusen/Getty Images; 30: S Curtis/Shutterstock; 31: Hero Images/Getty Images.